PERSUASIVE PRESE

Forthcoming titles in this series will include

- Winning Negotiation Tactics!
- Basic Business Finance!
- Successful Business Planning!
- Winning CVs!
- Getting Hired!
- Managing People for the First Time!
- Successful Interviewing Techniques!
- Letter Writing for Winners!
- Winning Telephone Techniques!

Do you have ideas for subjects which could be included in this exciting and innovative series? Could your company benefit from close involvement with a forthcoming title?

Please write to David Grant Publishing Limited
80 Ridgeway, Pembury, Tunbridge Wells, Kent TN2 4EZ
with your ideas or suggestions.

PERSUASIVE PRESENTATIONS

Michael James

60 Minutes Success Skills Series

Copyright © David Grant Publishing Limited 1997

First published 1997 by
David Grant Publishing Limited
80 Ridgeway, Pembury, Kent TN2 4EZ United Kingdom

60 Minutes Success Skills Series is an imprint of
David Grant Publishing Limited

All rights reserved. Except for the quotation of short passages for the purposes of criticism and review, no part of this publication may be reproduced, stored in a retrieval system, or transmitted, in any form or by any means, electronic, mechanical, photocopying, recording or otherwise, without the prior permission of the publisher.

British Library Cataloguing in Publication Data
A CIP catalogue record for this book is available from the British Library

ISBN 1-901306-03-8

Cover design: Steve Haynes

Text design: Graham Rich

Production editor: Paul Stringer

Typeset in Futura by
Archetype, Stow-on-the-Wold
http://ourworld/compuserve.com/homepages/Archetype

Printed and bound in Great Britain by
T.J. International, Padstow, Cornwall

This book is printed on acid-free paper

CONTENTS

Welcome: About *Persuasive Presentations* 7

Chapter 1: Planning the perfect presentation 11
    What makes a presentation persuasive
    The secret's in the planning
    Knowing what you want to say
    Understanding your audience
    How to plan a persuasive presentation

Chapter 2: Preparing perfect visuals 19
    Why you need good visuals
    Choosing the best visuals
    Getting the most from 35mm slides
    Wowing an audience with OHP transparencies
    Making the most of whiteboards and flipcharts
    Tips for preparing perfect visuals

Chapter 3: The secrets of good delivery 31
    Anyone can do it – even you!
    Winning over your audience
    Nerve-busting techniques
    Starting off
    Keeping them interested
    Tactics for good delivery

Chapter 4: Mastering the equipment 41
    Using an overhead projector
    Using a 35mm slide projector
    Using whiteboards and flipcharts
    Multi-media presentations
    How to master the equipment

Chapter 5: The big day! 51
    Rehearsing the part
    When to arrive
    Checking the room

Dealing with awkward customers
Planning a presentation in a hurry
Tips for the big day

Presentation planner 59

Welcome

ABOUT *PERSUASIVE PRESENTATIONS!*

Can you learn to wow your audience and give an effective presentation – and learn how to in just one hour? The answer is a resounding 'Yes'.

The only bit of waffle in the book

This book is part of the '60 Minutes Success Skills Series'. The series is written for people with neither the time nor patience to trawl through acres of jargon, management-speak and page-filling waffle. Many people would have you believe that giving a first-class presentation is incredibly difficult – or that it's something best left to the experts. In fact making a persuasive presentation is all about technique – skills that you can learn to develop quickly and easily.

This book recognises that time is precious. Like all the books in the series, it is founded on the belief that you can learn all you really need to know quickly and without fuss. The aim is to distil the essential, practical advice you can use straight away.

What do we mean by 'presentation'

In this book, the term presentation is used to describe any situation in which you have to talk to other people and get some kind of message across. This extends from surviving a job interview or convincing your bank manager that your request for an interest-free £50,000 overdraft is entirely reasonable, to standing up in front of an entire organisation to explain your plans for expansion and world domination.

In the job interview, the message you are putting over is that the job has your name written on it. Obviously, it would in most cases not be appropriate to wheel in a slide projector and erect a huge screen, but there are parallels. Instead of slides, your visual aids in an interview are your appearance and demeanour, and perhaps a portfolio of your work plus an arresting c.v.

The examples chosen for this book are from the middle ground. The same principles apply, no matter what sort of presentation you are faced with.

Is this book for you?

Persuasive Presentations! is packed full of useful and practical guidance for those who quiver at the very thought of standing up in front of others. You may have an excellent product or service to offer, or an exciting proposal to make, but can you sell it? How many times do you kick yourself for not making the best case for your ideas?

This book is for you if you find that:

- *you hate even the thought of giving a presentation;*
- *when you do give a presentation, you are often tongue-tied, dry-mouthed and nervous;*
- *your audience (whether it's one person or a hall-full) seems to be bored, or their attention wanders;*
- *you can't seem to get on with the equipment – overhead projectors, 35mm slide projectors, TV and video always seem to go wrong, ruining your presentation;*
- *you are ashamed of your visuals – your slides, transparencies, drawings, plans etc. all look a mess;*
- *you are competent – but you want to be better.*

Does any of this sound familiar? If so, this quick, no-bull guide to making persuasive presentations is just what you need. Read on.

Persuasive Presentations! offers you all the skills you'll need to make a perfect presentation to others. Take 60 minutes to find out how to wow your audience.

How to use this book

The message in this book is: 'It's OK to skim'. You don't have to read it all at once, or follow every tip to the letter. *Persuasive Presentations!* has been written to dip into so feel free to flick through to find the help you most need. It is a collection of 'hands on' tips that will help you tackle your presentations in way that suits you best and which gives you maximum impact.

You will find that there are graphic features used throughout the book.

WELCOME

> This means 'Something to think about' – it sets the scene and identifies the problems by prompting you to think about situations which will instantly feel familiar. — **YOU?**

> With the problem diagnosed, these features give you an action plan – this will help you to get your own ideas in order. — **ACT!**

> This feature appears at the end of each chapter. It is a checklist which condenses all of the advice given throughout the chapter. Similar features appear within chapters which are overflowing with tips! — **TIPS ✓**

As you read through the book, you will come across lots of practical advice on how to make those perfect presentations. If you're really pushed for time, you can always flick to the tips feature at the ends of chapters – these are also a useful reminder when you come back to look at this book in the future.

Good luck!

PLANNING THE PERFECT PRESENTATION — Chapter 1

What's in this chapter for you

What makes a presentation persuasive
The secret's in the planning
Knowing what you want to say
Understanding your audience
How to plan a persuasive presentation

> *I've often come out of a business presentation thinking that I knew nothing more than when I started.*
> – Ken Jones, sales manager

> *I often have to give presentations to colleagues – I hate doing it. I get tongue-tied, sweaty and sound terrible. Even if the idea I'm presenting is a great one, I somehow manage to make it sound really boring.*
> – Jack Harvey, technical support assistant

How many times has your presentation been less than persuasive? What was it that let you down?

What makes a presentation persuasive

Many people really dread having to make presentations. It's the same with interviews – an interview is another kind of presentation, but the product is *you*. Do you always put across your idea or product, or yourself, in the best way? Think about it for a moment. Can you see where, if anywhere, you go wrong?

> *The commonest reason for poor presentations, in my experience, is poor planning. Most people I see don't have a clue about what they are trying to achieve – apart from just getting to the end of the session.*
> – Ken Jones

Any presentation should have a clear objective in mind. Here are some examples.

- To deliver a clear message about the product, service, person and so on.
- To impart important information to the audience.
- To overcome false impressions or prejudices.
- To enthuse the audience so that they continue to support you.
- To encourage the audience to work with you, and not against you.
- To persuade people to find out more about your product or service.
- To persuade people to buy your product or service.
- To enhance your career.

Persuasion is not just about encouraging people to buy or place an order. It is about getting people to see things from your point of view. This means that before you can persuade anyone about anything, you have to be able to persuade yourself. You will never make a persuasive presentation unless you:

- believe in the product or service;
- respect your audience;
- get a kick out of making a successful presentation – in other words, care about getting it right; and
- respect yourself.

> **ACT!**
>
> Before you even begin planning your presentation, make sure that you really do believe in what you are doing. If not, ask someone else to do it, drop the idea all together, or work harder at convincing yourself.

The secret's in the planning

> *" You won't make a persuasive presenter unless you've done the planning. Even if it's just a few minutes before a meeting, planning what you are going to do is essential. "*
> **– Mike Jansen, marketing manager**

Planning is the secret of persuasive presentation. Think of it as a military campaign (except the audience is not, usually, your enemy). For a full-blown presentation, you ideally should have at least two weeks to plan really effectively. Remember, even if time is limited, the more planning you do, the better it will be.

What needs to be planned?

PLANNING THE PERFECT PRESENTATION

- *What you want to achieve by the end of the presentation*
- *The key points to be made*
- *The story you are going to tell*
- *The room where you will give the presentation*
- *Who will be listening and watching you*
- *What visuals you will use*
- *When and how the visuals will be created*
- *What equipment you need*

> Prepare a simple schedule showing when you will do each of the tasks listed above. There is more advice about each of these points in the following chapters.

Knowing what you want to say

> ❝ Never go into a presentation without working out first what you want to achieve. Giving a presentation without clear, measurable objectives is like flying a plane without instruments – you're going to need a hell of a lot of luck to get out alive. ❞
> – **Fran Bayliss, experienced tourism presenter**

The more focused your objectives, the more likely you will be to achieve them. As an example, rather than simply say 'My objective is to make people like the product', you should tell yourself 'By the end of the session I will make at least three good sales leads, distribute brochures to everyone present, make at least two appointments, get at least one order . . .' and so on.

> Before making a presentation write down a list of objectives – what do you want to achieve by the end of the session? Remember – the more definite the objective, the easier it will be to plan the perfect presentation.

> ❝ These days I never, ever, go into a presentation without having a set of targets in mind. These targets are always measurable, too. ❞
> – **Ken Jones**

PERSUASIVE PRESENTATIONS!

OK, you know where you are going – but how do you get there? Once you have worked out your objectives, next make a list of all the key points you want to make during the presentation.

> **ACT!**
>
> Write a list of the key points you want to make and put them into a priority order. Make sure you cover them all, and cover them comprehensively. At the end of each, give a summary to reinforce them.

" *Whenever I'm giving a presentation, I start with the objective. It might, for instance, be to get four new sales leads. OK. Then I write down a list of the key points I need to make – the importance of good promotional literature, how to achieve maximum impact, why our company delivers the goods . . . Then I put them into priority order and make sure that I spend the appropriate time during the presentation on each point.* "

– **Fran Bayliss.**

Are your presentations often 'worthy but dull'? People the world over enjoy a smile, a joke or an amusing tale. Try to put something a little light-hearted into your presentation but make sure it illustrates the point you are trying to make. People tend to remember a good story or amusing anecdote, but only if it's relevant. If you tell a joke with no relevance to the subject, people will laugh (maybe) but may take your main message less seriously too.

There's no sure-fire formula, but here are some very useful tips from old hands. These will help you to plan what you are going to say.

> **TIPS**
>
> When planning your presentation:
>
> ❑ *Always prepare a rough draft of what you are going to say and write a list of the key points you want to make plus your objective/s.*

> ❏ Make a note of every point you think is relevant and then go through the draft again, weeding out unnecessary material. Tell a good story. Your presentation should have all the elements of a cracking good yarn. All good stories should tell the listener something about you – use lots of 'I' sentences.
> ❏ Make sure you have a beginning, a middle and an end.
> ❏ Begin with a headline or some other attention-grabbing sentence. And always introduce yourself early on.
> ❏ Develop your story with supporting facts, figures, problems encountered and overcome, and so on.
> ❏ Spread your key priority points over the whole presentation – not too many at once.
> ❏ End by summarising the key points made and by stressing your objectives. For example: 'So my key message to you today is . . .'

Understanding your audience

> " Giving a presentation is like being on stage – it's a performance. And to perform well, you must know something about your audience. "
> – **Fran Bayliss**

The chances are that you can find out quite a bit about your audience before the presentation. Always try to do as much research as possible.

- Who will be there?
- Do they want to see you or were they forced to attend?
- What responsibilities do they have?
- What's their level in the organisation?
- Are they decision-makers or will they have to persuade someone else?
- What will they expect from you?
- What do they already know?
- Will they all understand you – how technical can you, or should you, be?
- Are they likely to ask questions?

The more you know about your audience in advance, the more persuasive your presentation will be.

PERSUASIVE PRESENTATIONS!

Here are some things to avoid.

- *Talking down to an audience – people hate to be patronised.*
- *Showing that you know little or nothing about them. (At least know something about their company – what it does, where it is, etc.)*
- *Being totally unprepared for questions.*
- *Knowing nothing about their current mood or concerns.*

> *I once gave a cheery presentation to a bunch of marketing guys who had just been told that their company was about to fold.*
> **– Mark Burton, promotion consultant**

The most common problem with audiences is to misjudge the people who are attending. It is all too easy to talk down to an audience that may know more than you do. They may also have totally different expectations from you.

YOU? How often have you been to a presentation where the speaker clearly knew nothing about your needs, wishes or expectations? Don't fall into this trap yourself – it can transform a competent presentation into a lead balloon.

The secret here is to try and see things from the audience's viewpoint. What do they need to know? What language or level of complexity should you offer? Will they all have technical and other essential knowledge?

You should also share with the audience something about you. This can be an effective way of making them warm to you and what you have to say.

ACT! Prepare some background material about you and try to let the audience have this before the presentation. Also, find out about your audience well in advance to make sure you're on the same wavelength.

PLANNING THE PERFECT PRESENTATION

The first steps in investigating your audience and learning how to wow them should be:

- *Ask the organisers to send you, if possible, an attendance list and discuss with them the likely make up of the audience – what are their interests, backgrounds, expectations, etc?*
- *Prepare yourself to adapt to an audience that wants you to slow down, use fewer technical terms, explain things more clearly, etc. (Rather than relying on a rigid script you should aim to have more than one way of expressing your key points.)*
- *If it's your first time, try rehearsing the presentation in front of unbiased friends or relatives. What do they think? Can they understand you? Is it interesting?*

How to plan a persuasive presentation

If you have a presentation to plan, here are the key points to start with.

1. Persuade yourself that it is worth giving. Believing in your message is an essential factor in making it persuasive.
2. List your key objective/s and main points and put them into a priority order.
3. Write a rough draft of your presentation using all of your key points in the order you know will be best.
4. Structure it so you have a beginning, a middle and an end. Begin with a dramatic eye- or ear-catching statement; end with the key objective.
5. Devise some way of telling the audience about you.
6. Decide as early as possible what visual aids you will be using.
7. Find out about where the presentation will be held.
8. Find out all you can about who will be attending.
9. Rehearse the presentation until you are satisfied.

This well-tried and trusted approach will help you plan a presentation that is really persuasive and memorable.

Preparing Perfect Visuals

— Chapter 2

What's in this chapter for you

- *Why you need good visuals*
- *Choosing the best visuals*
- *Getting the most from 35mm slides*
- *Wowing an audience with OHP transparencies*
- *Making the most of whiteboards and flipcharts*
- *Tips for preparing perfect visuals*

> " *My subject is so interesting, I don't need fancy gimmicks like slides or transparencies.* "

This is a dangerous assumption. Even professional stand-up artists often make use of visual aids.

Why you need good visuals

It's true – a picture *can* paint a thousand words. Visuals can be an immensely powerful way of illustrating a point or ramming home a key message. The best presentations are often those that combine a crisp, clear message with punchy visuals. Yet some people still think of visual aids as some kind of gimmick or prop to keep bored audiences awake. If your audience does fall asleep, it won't be the visuals to blame – it will be you! Visual aids to any presentation are there as a means of enhancing the message, not replacing it.

> **Think back to presentations you have attended. Try to remember some of the really boring ones. What made them so dull? The chances are it was because the speaker couldn't communicate and didn't use stimulating visuals.**

Lack of communication is far and away the main reason why presentations fail. An audience can easily get turned off by having nothing to see, nothing to stimulate the mind, or by having to listen to an argument or case that they simply cannot follow. Visual aids should help to overcome all of these shortcomings.

PERSUASIVE PRESENTATIONS!

Visual aids give an audience:

- *something else to look at other than you (no matter how 'visually pleasing' you are, it is always a good idea to give an audience variety);*
- *a means of summarising a complex idea after the talk;*
- *light relief from concentrating only on a voice;*
- *a better chance of visualising an argument, problem or solution; and*
- *another source of stimulation – colours and images.*

Visual aids also help *you* by:

- *reminding you where you are in the presentation;*
- *encouraging you to prepare the presentation more thoroughly;*
- *making the experience more varied and interesting; and*
- *giving you a chance to break free from your notes and make contact with the audience.*

> " *I wouldn't even contemplate running a presentation without some visual support – even if it's a humble whiteboard. Visuals are essential in getting your message across.* "
> **– Lee Wilde, trainer**

Lee is entirely correct. Research has shown that the spoken word accounts for a relatively small proportion of what people take in. Hearing plays second fiddle to sight when it comes to comprehending ideas and information.

What has the biggest impact in terms of what audiences take in from a presentation?

- ☐ *Over 50 per cent comes from what they see.*
- ☐ *Between 30 and 40 per cent comes from what they hear.*
- ☐ *Under 10 per cent comes from the actual content of the talk.*

Visual aids can have a powerful effect on an audience. But be careful: visuals can be too flashy and confusing or too distracting and annoying.

PREPARING PERFECT VISUALS

> ❝ *A good visual is a fantastic prop; a bad one does more harm than good.* ❞
> — Lee Wilde

Poorly designed visuals can do major damage to any presentation. Here are some of the classic visual mistakes — make sure you avoid them!

- ○ *Dense paragraphs of badly photocopied text given out as notes.*
- ○ *Fading whiteboard markers that cannot be read.*
- ○ *Out-of-focus slides or ones that don't seem to have any relevance to the talk.*
- ○ *Slides or transparencies filled with indigestible facts, figures or text.*
- ○ *Badly designed visuals that make you and your product/service look amateurish.*
- ○ *Too much, or too little, colour.*

ACT! Always prepare some kind of visual to assist in your presentation and ask an unbiased observer to rate the visuals on impact, simplicity and attractiveness.

Choosing the best visuals

> ❝ *One of the most difficult things is choosing which visuals to use for specific presentations. In the old days, I only ever used flip charts. But that's being far too rigid. Flexibility is the key.* ❞
> — **Tess Shepherd, marketing assistant**

YOU? Suppose you had to give a presentation next month. What visual aids would you choose to use and why?

Let's look briefly at what visuals are available to the average presenter. We can divide these very roughly into low-tech and hi-tech:

Low-tech visuals:

○ *flipcharts*
○ *white/blackboards*
○ *printed notes*

Hi-tech visuals:

○ *slide projector*
○ *overhead projector (OHP)*
○ *video recorder*

> ❝ *The visual aid often chooses me. If a venue has a 35mm projector, I bring my slides; if it has an OHP, I rustle up a transparency; if nothing else, I take along a flipchart and some pens.* ❞
> **Andrew Carpenter, personnel manager**

This is not the best attitude. If you fall into this way of working, it really means that you haven't put enough thought into your presentation and how to put your message across most effectively.

> **ACT!** — You should never be ruled by equipment. The choice of visual aids should, where possible, come down to one golden rule: "Choose the Visuals that will Make the Best Impact."

The secret in choosing the best visual is to know what you want to achieve *and* to know the strengths and weaknesses of each type of visual aid. We will look at some of these in the following sections of this chapter.

Think about what you want the visual to do for you. Here are some possibilities – it can help you to:

○ *define terms or jargon, or explain a complex or difficult idea;*
○ *revisit or emphasise a point to check that the audience fully understands;*
○ *provide an illustration or example to show the audience precisely what you mean;*
○ *summarise a section of the talk so far, stressing the key points you want the audience to remember.*

PREPARING PERFECT VISUALS

> **Remember:**
>
> ❑ Always, always practise using equipment – even a whiteboard – before the presentation.
> ❑ Whatever visual you use, make sure it looks as professional as possible and it can be read easily from the back of the room.
> ❑ Don't overdo it – too many visuals can exhaust an audience.
> ❑ Try not to take up more than 75 per cent of the time on visuals (people are there to see you as well as your visuals).

Getting the most from 35mm slides

> " *I'm happiest using 35mm slides and a projector – after all, it's what we show the holiday snaps on.* "
> – **Tom Watson, sales assistant**

Despite Tom's confidence, not everybody is happy using a slide projector. Slide projector fears include:

○ the bulb blowing during the session;
○ a slide jam in the holder;
○ getting the slides in upside down, or the wrong way round;
○ people won't be able to see the screen.

These fears are very common – and all too often justified. But slides can add tremendous impact to your presentation even though the technology can be worrisome.

> The simple secret is: "Know Your Slide Projector." Practise using it until you fully understand it and have mastered its foibles.

> " *Never, ever, use a slide projector for the first time during a presentation. The application of Sod's Law will almost certainly mean that something will go wrong. Find time to practise or don't use it at all.* "
> – **Lee Wilde**

PERSUASIVE PRESENTATIONS!

Projectors using the standard 35mm transparency, with its small cardboard or plastic holder, are very common. They vary in type. The older, more primitive ones require you to feed in a new slide each time and take the old one out of the machine. This can be very distracting for you and the audience. Try to use the carousel type that can be pre-loaded with slides. These can also be operated by remote control units, which is good because you are not then trapped into standing near the projector with your back to the audience.

When to use slide projectors:

- *When you want to add a dash of colour to your presentation.*
- *When it is important for the image to be razor sharp.*
- *When it is important for your presentation to be given with the highest possible level of professionalism.*
- *When you are having to address a large audience.*
- *When you want to keep your visuals for a long time and use them frequently.*
- *When there is no need to update the material.*
- *Whenever you have the time to produce slides, it is always worth while – slides make a great impression.*
- *When it is acceptable to have the room darkened.*
- *When you are comfortable with the technology.*

What to put on your slide

Slides are excellent for colour photographs, graphics and crisp, concise text. Don't overcrowd your slide, make sure it is easily readable and not too garish. Now check out the tips below. For more advice on equipment, see Chapter Four.

How to produce effective slides:

- If using text only, put no more than 8–10 lines on the slide.
- Avoid fancy, tiring, unreadable typefaces. Text should be well spaced out, clear and easy to read.
- If using your own graphics and text, try to avoid having more than four colours on each slide.
- If you are taking your own slides – make sure that the subject is properly lit and the camera exactly in focus. If you aren't confident, get someone to do this for you. Use a tripod for the camera and the most professional lighting system you can buy, rent or borrow.

PREPARING PERFECT VISUALS

Wowing an audience with OHP transparencies

> ❝ *For me, the OHP is the mainstay of any presentation –
> I take my own wherever I go. The biggest plus is that the system is
> so flexible. I can prepare a good transparency an hour or so before
> the event if I need to.* ❞
> **– Roger Grayson, consultant**

Roger is typical of many experienced presenters: the overhead projector (OHP) is a popular and highly flexible system. OHPs themselves are usually sturdy and simple to operate.
The OHP magnifies and projects an image on to a large screen. You will find out more about the equipment in Chapter Four. OHPs use a special sheet of acetate (or other transparent material) that can be written or drawn on using special pens. Images can also be photocopied on to the acetates so that text, graphics and even photographs can be projected.
Consider using an OHP when:

- you need to give your presentation in normal light;
- it is important to face your audience;
- you want to draw or copy your own graphics;
- you want to show statistics as graphs, charts or tables;
- you want to add details to your visual aid as you speak; and
- when you want to illustrate a point by building up a visual stage by stage.

> ❝ *When I want to show a flow chart, I use a series
> of OHP transparencies that sit on top of each other. I add a
> new transparency each time I want to add a new stage
> to the flow chart.* ❞
> **– Roger Grayson**

This technique is known as 'overlaying'. OHPs are ideal for this. You can overlay graphics or text on the sheet underneath to build up a complete picture, or set of bullet point arguments.
OHP transparencies (confusingly, sometimes called 'slides') can be prepared in advance by hand, or using a photocopier.

> ❝ *For fairly informal sessions, I use the OHP like a notebook –
> writing points directly on to the acetate as I go.* ❞
> **– Roger Grayson**

PERSUASIVE PRESENTATIONS!

Unless you are really experienced and confident, it is best to avoid writing directly on the transparency as you are giving a presentation. Every stroke is magnified on screen so that the audience will soon see a nervously shaking hand, or sweaty fingerprints and smudges. You'll have to be certain your handwriting is legible too!

> **Using OHP transparencies to present text.**
>
> ❑ Make sure your letters are at least 8mm high (roughly 32 point on your wordprocessor) for an audience sitting up to 10 metres away from the screen. The further away the audience, the bigger the letters should be – 15mm and above.
> ❑ Use landscape (wide) format rather than portrait (long and narrow) whenever you can without having to change midway through. Leave a 30mm border around the edges.
> ❑ The most common fault on portrait OHP transparencies is to have too many words. Keep to no more than eight words per line and eight lines per page – as a rule of thumb, think 888: 8mm high letters, 8 words per line, 8 lines per sheet.
> ❑ Stick to neat, clear typefaces such as Helvetica or Ariel, and use capital letters very sparingly – TOO MANY CAPITALS CAN BE VERY TIRING ON THE EYES. Hand-written transparencies must be legible – print them, and do so carefully.
> ❑ Use attention-grabbing headlines, quotes or questions as often as you can. Think about the layout of each page – make sure it is interesting to look at.
> ❑ Put your key messages in the top two-thirds of the transparency.
> ❑ Don't leave too much blank (and, therefore, glaring) space – stick in an attractive graphic to liven things up.
> ❑ Write several drafts to make sure you cut out all unnecessary words and use bullet points to highlight lists.
> ❑ Never photocopy a transparency-filling page of statistics.
> ❑ Use coloured marker pens to add variety, highlight key words, etc.

PREPARING PERFECT VISUALS

Making the most of whiteboards and flipcharts

> *For a small group, you just cannot beat the immediacy of the good old-fashioned flip chart*
> – **Lee Wilde**

Flipcharts are still a mainstay of most business presentations. The attractions are obvious: they are cheap to buy and run, very portable and reliable. Flipcharts are usually mounted on an adjustable easel and can be positioned anywhere in a room.
  Flipcharts are especially useful when:

- *you want to get feedback from the audience – they allow you to write down ideas and suggestions;*
- *you are leading a brainstorming session;*
- *you want people to write down their own ideas;*
- *you want to encourage a relaxed, informal atmosphere.*

Flipcharts are often useful for quickly writing down ideas that can then be marshalled into some kind of order. They can also be prepared in advance so that you turn to a new sheet as the presentation progresses. This can be advantageous when:

- *there is a difficult graphic to draw;*
- *you want to provide a stimulus message – perhaps some thought-provoking question – at a certain point in your presentation;*
- *you don't have time to write down everything you need to as you go, or you don't have the confidence to write and speak at the same time.*

Here are some hints on how to use flipcharts to full effect.

- ❑ Prepare some of your flipcharts in advance but leave spaces to add ideas from the group. You can emphasise points by drawing boxes around the key words you've already written down.
- ❑ Always have a full supply of marker pens – at least three or four colours, with back-ups for each – and pins or tape to stick the charts to walls if need be.
- ❑ If you are writing during the presentation, buy the flipcharts with ruled paper to help guide your text.

TIPS

twenty-seven

PERSUASIVE PRESENTATIONS!

TIPS
- ❑ If drawing a chart during a session, prepare in advance by drawing faint, pencilled guide lines.
- ❑ Don't use newsprint – it tears too easily and the ink tends to run.
- ❑ Use a flipchart where most of what you want to show is text-based.
- ❑ Make sure your writing is clear enough to be legible from the back of the hall – as a rough guide, keep your lettering at least 30mm high. Print your text but don't overuse capital letters and never write in longhand
- ❑ Stick to another rule of eights – no more than eight lines per page and avoid writing in the bottom eighth of the page (it is probably out of sight for some people, unless you are speaking in a tiered auditorium).

There are times when flipcharts should be avoided. Find an alternative if:

- ○ you are speaking to a large group, perhaps 35 or more – they can be difficult to see from the back of a large hall;
- ○ the results of a group discussion need to be copied – flipcharts are usually too large for most photocopiers;
- ○ you need to make a really top-quality presentation and use complex graphics.

Whiteboards

Much of what has been said for flipcharts also applies to using whiteboards. Like flipcharts, they really come into their own in small group discussions where you are trying to extract ideas from the audience. The boards provide a clean, white surface that allows text and graphics to be very clearly seen. Any mistakes or amendments can quickly be dealt with by wiping off the existing text.

TIPS

If you are using a whiteboard:

- ❑ Always carry spare marker pens – and keep the tops on them because they dry out very quickly.
- ❑ Carry a range of colours and nib thicknesses. Try green, navy blue, black, red and orange markers rather than pinks, light blues and, especially, yellows. Strong colours are easier to see from a distance.

PREPARING PERFECT VISUALS

> ❑ *Have a damp cloth or sponge at the ready to clean the board thoroughly.*
> ❑ *Use a yellow fine-nibbed pen to draw guide lines to keep your text straight and upright.*
> ❑ *Practise writing on the whiteboard before your presentation begins.*

Only use a whiteboard in a fairly small room – no one should be more than 5 metres away from the board.

> " *I tend to use a whiteboard when my presentation can be clearly broken down into self-contained segments. I gradually fill a whiteboard to cover one segment. Then when we are ready to move on, I wipe the board clean.* "
> – **Denise Clinton, technology consultant**

Tips for preparing perfect visuals

You should always support your presentation with visuals. Here are some suggestions that will make it easier to produce visual aids that work for you.

1. Think carefully about what you want the visual to do for you (for instance, helping you to define terms or to emphasise your key points) before you start.
2. Practise using whatever equipment you intend to use – even a whiteboard – before the presentation.
3. If you are using an overhead projector (OHP) or a flipchart, prepare as much as you can before the event. Don't leave yourself with too much writing or drawing to do while you are speaking – it can distract the audience and interrupt the flow of your presentation.
4. Make sure the presentation looks as professional as possible and that all visual aids can be seen easily from everywhere in the room. Eye-catching graphics, logos and illustrations will make your talk more authoritative.

TIPS

5. Don't use too many visuals, and leave even gaps in between – a long stream of visuals without explanation or enough time to absorb them will turn the audience off. Depending on their complexity, a viewer-friendly rate is one visual every five minutes. Always speak while showing them.
6. Avoid fancy, tiring, unreadable typefaces. Text should be clear and east to read. Make sure your hand-written aids are legible. Use capital letters sparingly.
7. Try not to pack too much text on to one page or slide – as a rule of thumb, think eight words per line, eight lines per page.
8. Put your key messages in the top two-thirds of an OHP transparency. Think about the layout of each page – make sure it is interesting to look at.
9. Use colour for emphasis or to liven up graphs and charts – but always sparingly.
10. Use overlays to build up an argument or a complete picture. You can buy special transparency pads to make sure that each slide is exactly in line with the ones underneath it.

These simple guidelines will help you prepare cracking visuals every time.

THE SECRETS OF GOOD DELIVERY — Chapter 3

What's in this chapter for you

Anyone can do it – even you!
Winning over your audience
Nerve-busting techniques
Starting off
Keeping them interested
Tactics for good delivery

> *" The thought of standing up in front of others used to turn me to jelly. "*
> – Joe Riley, project engineer

Does that sound familiar? For so many people, there is nothing more terrifying than standing up in front of others (usually strangers) to give a talk, lecture or presentation.

Anyone can do it – even you!

Most people are scared by the thought of public speaking. Their fears are very common.

- What if I dry up?
- What if the audience hates me?
- What if my equipment fails?
- What if I get a really difficult question or an aggressive member of the audience?

Making a presentation is an art – but it's one that can be learnt. It all comes down to communication. When presenting an idea, product, service, a research paper – it doesn't matter what the subject matter is – the way you communicate is paramount. For those who have not prepared properly, it's usually the case that they:

- can't be heard and seen properly;
- can't be understood;
- can't keep their audience interested or awake.

YOU? — Think of a really poor presentation you have attended. Can you see where the speaker went wrong?

To make a real impact there has to be *both* a strong message and good delivery. You cannot rely on message alone; neither is it effective to have an all-singing, all-dancing delivery with no message.

Effective delivery is all about technique. True, some people are naturally more confident, have louder voices or are natural crowd pleasers. But, as you will see, even the most shy individuals can learn how to deliver well.

YOU? — What, in your opinion, are your main shortcomings as a presenter? Is your voice too quiet or sleep-inducingly monotonous? Do you get nervous and flustered?

Whatever problems you identify in your delivery technique, there is a cure. For example:

- *If your voice is too quiet, try learning the techniques of voice projection or use a microphone.*
- *If your voice is monotonous, learn about voice modulation and use a lot of visuals to add variety.*
- *If you get terribly nervous, remember that being a presenter is like acting – so learn the role and rehearse the part. You'd be amazed how this will boost your confidence.*

ACT! — If your audience is likely to exceed 15 people, always try to use a microphone (or at least have one standing by).

Winning over your audience

> " *Once you realise that an audience is not your enemy, making a presentation becomes much easier.* "
>
> – **Joe Riley**

THE SECRETS OF GOOD DELIVERY

It's true – an audience can make or break your presentation. Standing up in front of others is just like giving a stage performance. You'll need to use some of the techniques of trained actors – like them you must prepare for your performance.

> *The first few minutes are crucial – the audience will make up its mind whether to listen to you or switch off.*
> – **Joe Riley**

Joe's right – the first impressions of a presenter are lasting impressions.

As we saw in Chapter One, an effective tactic is to understand your audience. This means that you should do some research before a presentation. Remember to ask:

- Who will be there? Try to get names, titles, responsibilities, etc.
- What level are they? Are they decision-makers, opinion-formers, people of influence?
- What do they already know? What level of technical knowledge can you assume?
- What are they expecting of me?

The more you know about them, the easier it is to begin the presentation in the right way and make that all-important good first impression.

Make sure you have an accurate picture of your audiences and their expectations before each presentation you are asked to give.

ACT!

> *I recently gave a lecture on timber drying to an audience which I assumed was composed of saw mill managers. I used quite a lot of technical terms and engineering jargon. Only afterwards did I realise that most of my audience were Russians who understood only basic English – and they were shippers not loggers – whoops!*
> – **Roger Aitken, timber consultant**

If you can, it is also wise to find out what went on before your presentation. Find out what mood the audience is likely to be in. If you know that your audience has had a long, rather tiring morning, and your presentation is just before lunch, keep it short and light. Remember that, according to research, people's attention span is limited to 20 minutes, but if they are hungry and tired it will be even shorter.

> **ACT!** Try to time your presentation just after morning coffee when the audience is still alert and 'warmed up'. Avoid, if you can, slots just before lunch, just after lunch or late in the day.

Nerve-busting techniques

Before you appear before any audience, it helps if you have the basic techniques of nerve-busting at your disposal:

- *Calming.* Before going on, close your eyes, take at least ten deep breaths. One long breath in, hold it for 10 seconds, and a slow release. Repeat this and try to concentrate only on getting your breath into a nice, slow rhythm.
- *Relaxing.* Try these simple muscle relaxing techniques – clench both fists really tight and then release. Screw up your face muscles tight, then release. Repeat this at least five times before starting your presentation.
- *Focusing.* Banish all thoughts out of your head except the presentation. Imagine while you are up there that nothing else in the world is going on – no worries at home, no parking problems, no dread of a forthcoming visit to the dentist.
- Try to talk to members of the audience before your presentation. Meet them over coffee or in the registration period. If you know two or three people, just imagine you are talking exclusively to them.
- Take a drink just before starting. Drink little sips of water (never alcohol, which will slow you down and make things worse later). Keep a glass of water nearby to keep your mouth from drying up.

> " Before my presentations, I always give myself a couple of minutes to compose myself – a bit of deep breathing to help me relax and clear my mind of everything except what I'm about to do. It really helps. "
> **– Lee Wilde, trainer**

As you prepare yourself, try always to keep at the back of your mind what audiences love. They will warm to you if:

THE SECRETS OF GOOD DELIVERY

- *They can hear every word, even at the back.*
- *They are made to feel welcome.*
- *You address them in relaxed way, showing you are happy to be there.*
- *The presentation is shorter than they expect.*
- *Your presentation uses a careful mix of voice and visuals.*
- *You dish out one or two jokes or funny anecdotes (that are relevant).*
- *You address them on a personal level*

Once you arrive on the podium, or whatever, it is important to make the audience feel relaxed.

Relaxing your audience means appearing relaxed yourself. So:

- *Walk slowly and deliberately to your place.*
- *Take your time launching into your presentation – smile gently, make all your actions deliberate ones. If you fumble, laugh it off or make it look 'part of the act'.*
- *Put your hands in your pockets if they are shaking or sweating – but don't jangle keys, coins or anything else you've got in there.*
- *Work at looking relaxed – it's all part of the act, and very soon it will become a natural state of mind.*

TIPS

Starting off

> " *The worst time in a presentation is the first few minutes. If you get off to a bad start it's almost impossible to recover. But a good start can cover for any number of errors later.* "
> **– Roger Aitken**

One of the most annoying things for any audience is a speaker who cannot be heard. Not only is this frustrating, but it is often taken as a sign that the speaker neither knows nor cares much about his/her audience. This is the worst possible start.

TIPS

Can't be heard? Here's what to do.

- *If you have a naturally quiet voice, consider using a microphone, even with a small audience. (NB always practise with a microphone before you use it. If hand-held, hold it tightly and rigidly just under your mouth, a few centimetres away. Check volume levels and avoid feedback by keeping it away from a speaker.)*
- *Where there is a small audience, try to arrange the seating so that no one is too far away (there's more on this in Chapter Five).*
- *Test out your voice projection with a friend. From how far away can you be heard without a microphone?*
- *Practise voice projection. Fill your lungs and try to speak from your diaphragm rather than your throat. Ask a singer or voice coach in your local theatre group how to do this if you need help.*
- *Target a couple of members of the audience at the very back of the room and make sure that your voice carries to them. Look at their body language – can they hear you?*
- *Check straight away with the audience – "Can you hear me?" Don't wait for someone to shout out "Speak up!" – by that stage you will have lost their good will.*

Start with a bang

It is vital to set the right tone straight away. Remember that first impressions count. You've arrived on stage: smile at the audience and look enthusiastic; greet them and then, if you need to, introduce yourself – name, position, brief (very brief) summary of why you are here and what makes you qualified to speak on this subject. Start the presentation proper with some kind of dramatic opener. Here are some that others have tried.

- *Firing a starting gun into the air.*
- *"From this morning, your life is about to change forever."*
- *"Ladies and gentleman, I'm hear to talk about death. The death of an old idea."*
- *"I'm going to begin with something rather shocking (dramatic pause) – Electricity."*

You will obviously need to choose something that suits your own audience, but do find some way to get their interest. *Don't* start by:

- showing a lengthy video clip;
- reading from notes;
- apologising for taking up their time.

Make contact; grab their attention immediately.

> **Here's a typical opener.**
>
> - *Start with a short thank you to the Chair for introducing you, if that's appropriate.*
> - *Break the ice with a few words of welcome such as "Thank you very much for coming to my presentation today. I hope you find it interesting and useful . . ."*
> - *Set the scene with a short summary of what the presentation is about and what you hope to achieve by the end.*
> - *Give any practical details – when the session will end, arrangements to follow, when and where questions will be encouraged.*
> - *Cast your hook. Grab their attention*

Keeping them interested

Always be aware of your audience. Try not to make the room constantly so dark, or the lighting so dazzling, that you lose precious eye contact. An audience will send out all kinds of body language signals which will tell you whether they are bored, interested or hanging on your every word.

> *" It's easy to tell if the audience is interested in what you are saying. Watch out for their body language. Are they shuffling in their seats too much? Are they yawning or fidgeting? Are they staring out of the window or looking at their watches? "*
> – **Kate Cohen, fashion designer**

Try at all times to maintain eye contact with different people in the audience. Don't look over their heads or, worse, out of the window.

Keeping in touch with your audience is the best way to gauge their interest in your presentation. If you've structured your talk in as lively and interesting a way as possible, you shouldn't go wrong. Feedback from the audience will tell you how you're doing.

To keep an audience with you, think of your presentation as a story. The best stories keep listeners attentive for hours.

> **TIPS**
>
> Learn from the great storytellers. Begin by writing an outline of what you are going to say. Here is a simple standard outline:
>
> - *Welcome the audience and introduce yourself.*
> - *Set the scene – tell the audience why they are here, where they are heading (thanks to your presentation) and how progress can be made thanks to your ideas.*
> - *Develop the main nub of your argument – keep to the key points, cut waffle.*
> - *Recommend action to be taken.*
> - *Give a short summary of the key points and thank the audience for attending.*
> - *Invite questions from the floor.*

Once your outline is written, flesh it out. Then cut it by 10 per cent. Then cut it again and again until only the absolute essentials are there. Experienced presenters tend to err on the side of brevity. Remember – nobody loves a windbag.

> *" I always include some stories about my personal 'on-stage' disasters in my training presentations. Not only do they get a laugh, they reinforce my points in a powerful way and keep the audience hooked. "*
>
> – **Rufus Paul, product demonstrator**

Think of the presentation as a conversation (albeit one-sided) between you and people you know. It's a story. Use the benefits of your own, personal experience. Use humour whenever you can, but keep it part of the story – if people smile or laugh, it tells you they are listening. Your visuals can help you to keep their interest, too, but keep them simple and fully a part of what you are saying. Don't let them divert the audience's attention from you.

Prompts

Remember, every good story should have a beginning, a middle and an end. And that's the order in which you should deliver it. Wrtite down notes to stop you straying from your running order. Keep them brief – *never* bury your head in a script. Maintain constant eye contact with different members of the audience.

> Write down your key points on a set of postcard-sized cards. These "card prompts" allow you to keep eye contact with your audience and running through them in order will keep you right on track.

You can also keep the audience's attention by asking them questions, inviting them to contribute ideas or pass on their experiences. (But, if you are asking for contributions from the audience, beware of common pitfalls. Make sure that the person can be heard or repeat the question or comment. Do not let a member of the audience hog the limelight or ramble on – the others will resent him/her and you for allowing it to happen.)

Tactics for good delivery

> Good delivery is key to a persuasive presentation. To improve your technique, work on these golden rules.
>
> 1. Learn to use nerve-busting techniques and focus your mind just before a presentation.
> 2. Use a microphone if the audience is above 15 or you have a naturally quiet voice. Practise projecting your voice too.
> 3. Find out as much as you can about the audience in advance – tailor your talk to their specific needs (language, technical level etc.).
> 4. Try to get the 'plum' spot in the day – after a morning break is a good time.

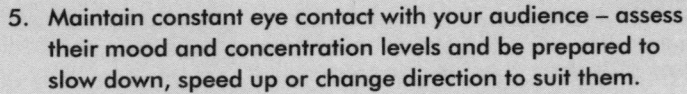

TIPS

5. Maintain constant eye contact with your audience – assess their mood and concentration levels and be prepared to slow down, speed up or change direction to suit them.
6. Introduce yourself and establish a rapport. Even if you're not, try to appear calm and happy to be there. Smile.
7. Begin dramatically – grab their attention. End with a 'thank you'.
8. Structure your talk like a good story, with a beginning, a middle and an end, and add a personal element whenever possible.
9. Use humour – but sparingly and only when it fits in with your message.
10. Avoid pompous language or 'written' style of speaking. Talk in the way you would to a friendly colleague.
11. Remember KISS – Keep It Simple, Stupid!

Follow these easy-to-learn principles and you will soon be giving excellent presentations, every time.

MASTERING THE EQUIPMENT — Chapter 4

What's in this chapter for you

> Using an overhead projector
> Using a 35mm slide projector
> Using whiteboards and flipcharts
> Multi-media presentations
> How to master the equipment

> " *I used to be really scared of the equipment I used in a presentation. I could never relax – Will I know what to do if a slide gets stuck? What if the bulb blows? What if no one can see the chart or if the whiteboard's too dirty.* "
> **– Mike Collins, MD of an engineering firm**

This chapter is for anyone who thinks of machinery as the enemy. It's also for those who can't see that presentation equipment is really to help not hinder the event.

Using an overhead projector

One of the most common pieces of equipment used in presentations is the overhead projector (OHP) – basically a glorified magnifying glass.

Have you ever sat cringing while an ill-prepared presenter, in a whirlwind of fluttering transparencies, assails your eyes with back to front or miniscule words, which were out of focus in the first place? Don't follow suit – OHPs are simple and effective if used properly.

Like all pieces of machinery, an overhead projector responds to careful handling, is best used by those who know how to use it and, yes, does occasionally go wrong. The key to mastering an OHP is confidence.

> " *Now I use OHPs, slides, flipcharts, the lot . . . with total confidence. The secret is to know what you're doing beforehand – I learned a lot from my mistakes, the rest just by practising.* "
> **– Mike Collins**

PERSUASIVE PRESENTATIONS!

Let's begin by choosing your OHP, although of course, in many cases, the OHP will be chosen for you. But let's suppose that you do have some control. If you intend to make frequent presentations, it is definitely worth having your own equipment.

How to choose an OHP

- *Make sure all the controls (for instance, the 'on/off' switch) are visible and can be operated easily from where you are standing.*
- *If you are always on the move, choose one of the lighter, portable machines – some are under 5kg, although they have a less powerful light.*
- *If brightness of image is a key requirement (for instance, when it is necessary to present your talk in full daylight), use a projector with a power rating of at least 400W. (They can go up to 500W.)*
- *Choose a model with twin lamps – then if one bulb blows you can change it without fuss.*
- *Check out the fan noise. On some models, it can be significant but on most it is barely audible.*

Once you have switched on the OHP there are two possible adjustments to make:

- *The focus knob – usually a large, knurled knob on the side of the OHP. As you turn it, the image should become more or less in focus.*
- *A swivel lens – this helps you adjust the height of the image as it is projected on to the screen. Notice that the higher up you project the image, the more distorted it tends to be. This is known as the 'keystone distortion'. It can be reduced by varying the angle of the projector screen itself.*

If possible, adjust both of these things before the presentation begins.

ACT! — If you have to adjust the height and focus in front of the audience, try to involve them. Using a trial transparency, ask some of them whether they can read the slide in full. This will help to keep their attention.

When you have finished talking about the image projected on the screen, either move on to the next or switch the OHP off.

MASTERING THE EQUIPMENT

Never leave the OHP switched on when you don't need it: it will only be a distraction. This is doubly true if there is no transparency to be shown. You risk dazzling the audience (with bright light rather than your expertise).

Using 'film'

Rather confusingly, the sheets you put on the OHP go by several names: 'film', 'transparencies', 'acetates' or, sometimes, 'slides'. For now, we will stick to film. You can buy two kinds:

- Write-on film – *this is made from acetate or PVC and is designed to be written on with a special marker pen. You can create your own hand-written text or graphics.*
- Photocopy film – *this is a heavier-duty film, especially designed for different sorts of photocopiers, dot matrix, bubblejet, inkjet, and laser printers.*

Here are some tips on OHP film.

- Never put 'write-on' film into a photocopier – *you are likely to damage both.*
- There is a huge variety of film on offer – *make sure you have one that's compatible with your printer or photocopier.*
- Choose a heavier film if you want to make a large number of copies.
- For variety, use coloured film.

TIPS

Choosing a screen

> *" I've found to my cost that to show a really crisp and sharp image on an OHP, you also have to have a good, white screen. "*
> – **Fiona Tollard, trainer**

Have you suffered a presentation (or even a slide show) on a makeshift screen – a curtain that just won't stay still, or a wall covered with woodchip? You know Fiona's right.

YOU?

forty-three

PERSUASIVE PRESENTATIONS!

Whether you are going to buy your own screen or merely checking the facilities ahead of your talk, there are some cardinal rules in choosing and using screens:

- Make sure you can carry the screen if you need to.
- Practice erecting it – if it's not quick and easy to put up or fold, you might inadvertently give your audience a slapstick display.
- Make sure it's very stable (possibly another laugh at your expense).
- Make sure it can be tilted to counteract 'keystone distortion'.

TIPS

Getting the most from an OHP and screen . . .

- Follow the 1:6 rule for screen size and distance from the audience. If the screen is 1 metre square, the audience should be no further than 6 metres away from it; 12m for a 2m screen, and so on.
- Position the screen at the most comfortable height for the average viewer. The best angle from viewer to screen is about 40 degrees above the horizontal line of sight.
- Check that everybody can see the whole screen. If not, raise and tilt the screen downwards (or make sure that no important message goes in the bottom quarter of the transparency). Check seats at the front and the back of the room in advance if you can, and assume the audience are all tall and sporting bouffants.

Using a 35mm slide projector

" It's every presenter's nightmare – putting the slides in upside down and wrong way round, getting them in the wrong order and a bulb blowing half way through your 'Seven Wonders of Wet Fish Preserving' talk. "
— **Fiona Tollard**

It's certainly true that 35mm slide projectors are notoriously troublesome. It seems that all the gremlins in the universe want to get at your machine – only on the day of the talk, of course. Yet with a little planning, every problem can be overcome. Using a slide projector is actually very easy once you get the hang of it.

There are many different makes and models but when choosing a projector try to get the following features:

MASTERING THE EQUIPMENT

- A remote control button for moving slides along is a must – it allows you to keep looking at the audience rather than fiddling about with the projector.
- A remote control feature for focusing. This, too, saves a lot of bending over a hot, dimly lit projector and distracting the audience.
- A magazine or carousel loading mechanism. These are normally detachable so that the slides can be inserted before the presentation.

A carousel-type loading system is the best but make sure you can at least half fill it. Any less than this and it's not really worth using slides and a projector.

Again, preparation leads to success. Load your slides before the presentation making sure that, when projected, they are the right way round and the correct way up. Practise doing this until you can do it quickly and accurately. Try to make time for a trial run – it's easy to overlook things if you're hurried.

Here are some tips on using slide slides and projectors:

- Mark each slide with a pencilled number – this will help you get them in the right order, especially if you drop them.
- Put a blank, opaque slide in if there is to be a break in the flow of slides – this saves you from having to switch off each time (thus shortening the life of the bulb). It also saves the audience from having to stare at a dazzlingly blank screen.
- Don't present your talk in total darkness – have a spotlight on you or switch on main lights after each cluster of slides has been shown. If you have to be in the dark, make sure you can see your notes – a small lectern light or anglepoise lamp, for instance.
- If a slide does get stuck, don't panic. Calmly put on the house lights and try to reload the slide – or apologise, and move on to the next one.
- Use glass-mounted slides for longer life and keep your fingerprints off them. Don't store them in the carousel or in a cold room (or on a scorching-hot car seat).

TIPS

Using whiteboards and flipcharts

These may be the 'low-tech' end of the presentations market, but whiteboards and flipcharts can be ideal in certain situations. They come in all shapes and sizes. At the top end, you can buy whiteboards with built-in photographic scanners that can make instant photocopies of the board's contents. This is invaluable for handouts as once the whiteboard is wiped clean, the product of your labour is gone forever. At the more modest end of the market is the simple whiteboard and flipchart. Here are some pointers to help you choose:

Choosing a flipchart easel and pad

- Make sure the easel height can be easily adjusted up to about 175cm.
- Make sure the easel is stable once assembled. Remember, you will be tearing sheets off the pad – often in a hurry.
- The easel should have a sturdy hook system on which to hang the pad – and it should be easy to hang and take down the pad.
- The easel should be able to hold two pads and a pen tray.
- Use a top quality cartridge paper – the ink often spreads on cheap, newsprint-type pads.
- Make sure that the paper is well perforated so that it can be easily torn off

Choosing a whiteboard

- Get a board that fits the space you have available – there are many shapes and sizes.
- Get one with ready-marked grids to help guide your text and graphics.
- Make sure it is easy to wipe and clean.
- Make sure it is scratch resistant.

With your flipchart and/or whiteboard in place, the next thing to consider is the marker pens.

> **"** There is nothing more irritating for an audience than trying to read faint or pale text written with an old, dried-up marker pen. **"**
>
> **– Mike Collins**

Glance through any stationery catalogue and you will find an enormous variety of marker pens. They are designed specifically for flipchart or whiteboard use. Flipchart pens normally contain water-based inks designed to dry quickly and not smudge. You can also buy pens for the flipchart which are fade resistant, free of squeaks (a boon to audiences) and which do not bleed ink on to

MASTERING THE EQUIPMENT

the unused page below. The ink from whiteboard pens is designed to be wiped clean.

For both whiteboard and flipchart pens, look out for those with:

- the widest range of colours, including fluorescent ones; and
- the largest choice of nibs and line widths – then you can do anything from chunky, bold lines to the finest strokes.

How to get the most from your whiteboard/flipchart:

- Make sure it can be seen clearly – even from the back.
- If using a flipchart, consider sticking torn-off completed sheets around the room. This can be very useful for summarising group discussions or progress made.
- Use the correct marker pens designed for the job – for instance, don't use a permanent marker pen on a whiteboard.
- Clean whiteboards as soon as you have finished – the longer you leave it, the harder it is to do.
- When cleaning a whiteboard, use a slightly damp cloth rather than a dry wiper. Give the board an occasional clean with a proprietary board cleaner – or try a small amount of diluted bleach and water.
- Use strong dark colours such as black, blue, red and green. Yellows, light purples and browns are more difficult to see.

TIPS

Multi-media presentations

> " Don't think of each type of equipment as exclusive to one set of circumstances. Variety is always good and I try to use at least an OHP **or** slide projector with a flipchart **or** whiteboard. "
> – **Mike Collins**

It's true that you should not see each piece of equipment in isolation. Consider using two or more media – it will help to liven up your presentation and help you to play to your strengths. Each visual aid has its place. When choosing what equipment to use, consult the following guidelines.

PERSUASIVE PRESENTATIONS!

OHPs – when and why

Overhead projectors can be useful with both large and small audiences. They allow you to:

- Build up a picture or argument stage by stage.
- Get ideas from the audience and record them next to yours.
- Show charts, graphs, statistics, and plot the trends without defacing the original.
- Highlight key words or phrases, and again keep the source intact.

35mm slides – when and why

These are best used with large audiences. They are ideal for:

- Showing photographs of people and places, things you can't reproduce and present in other ways.
- Displaying high-quality graphics or complex drawings.

Flipcharts – when and why

Flipcharts work really well with small audiences. Use them when you want to:

- Run informal discussions.
- Take lots of ideas from the audience and display them throughout the presentation.
- Summarise selected ideas or questions from the audience.

Whiteboards – when and why

Whiteboards are best used with small audiences. They are good for:

- Quickly recording a limited number of ideas at any one time.
- Showing how graphs, charts, flow diagrams, etc. are built up or drawn.

YOU? — Can you see the areas of overlap? The shared advantages of each in particular situations can be used together in a multi-media presentation.

forty-eight

MASTERING THE EQUIPMENT

Examples of mixed media presentations

You could, for example, use an OHP transparency to introduce ideas and concepts and then use a flipchart to elicit and record the audience's ideas. Next, you could write down key points that emerge on an OHP transparency laid on top of your first one.

Or, you could begin by stimulating your audience with top quality photographs shown on 35mm slides. The key learning points can then by summarised on OHP transparencies as they unfold. Flipcharts situated within the audience could be used to write down ideas generated by small groups.

You should be able to find an effective combination to suit any presentation you have to make.

Keep these tips in mind as you prepare.

- *If using an OHP and a flipchart, put the OHP in the centre of your area.*
- *Put the flipchart to one side (depending on which hand you use for writing) so you don't have to stand directly in front of it as you write.*
- *Make sure that the flipchart and OHP screen can be seen clearly from the back of the audience.*
- *If using a 35mm slide projector, set it up in advance and give yourself plenty of time before the presentation to check all slides, positioning and controls.*
- *Think about lighting – put the flipchart near a source of natural light and whatever screen you're using in a darker corner.*

How to master the equipment

All you have to do to master your equipment is live by these rules:

1. Choose an OHP to suit your needs – portable, standard, or extra powerful for daylight presentations.
2. Practise using all controls on the OHP or slide projector. Find out how to switch on and off, how to change bulbs,

PERSUASIVE PRESENTATIONS!

TIPS

3. Where possible, get a technician to set everything up for you – including checking the focus and screen position. If you have to do this yourself, do it well before the start of your talk.
4. Make sure in advance that your screen/flipchart is well positioned so that it can be seen easily from all parts of the room.
5. Be careful when choosing OHP film – make sure it is suitable for a photocopier, inkjet printer or writing on directly.
6. Don't dazzle the audience with bright light – switch the projector off or use opaque slides between the separate elements of your talk.
7. For very important presentations to large audiences, move Heaven and Earth to get a back-up projector in case something goes wrong.
8. Practise inserting slides into the projector, or transparencies on to the OHP – make sure you can consistently get them the right way up and not back to front.
9. Choose strong colours when using a flipchart/whiteboard and pens. Use flipcharts with high-quality paper and make sure all your pens work. Have a damp cloth at the ready to clean a whiteboard.

Follow these tips and you will soon learn to love the equipment you use in presentations.

THE BIG DAY!

— Chapter 5

What's in this chapter for you

Rehearsing the part
When to arrive
Checking the room
Dealing with awkward customers
Planning a presentation in a hurry
Tips for the big day

> " Like an actor, you need to have prepared for your role, learnt the script, practised handling the props with ease so that on the day all you need to do is make sure you don't bump into the furniture! "
> – Kay Fleming, marketing manager

It's true that giving a presentation is very much like giving a performance. However, if you've done the preparation it should be alright on the night.

Rehearsing the part

And now it's the day of the presentation. If you have followed the tips in this book you should by now have a finely tuned script, a powerful arsenal of visual aids to illustrate the points you want to make, and full mastery of your props.

> **YOU?** Has the hard work you put into preparing the talk left you feeling smugly confident? Good! Confidence is the best cure for nerves and the best antidote for Sod's Law.

The final hurdle is knowing your weakspots. You have to manage yourself through these while you're on stage. This involves keeping an eye on yourself – 'slow down, you're speaking too quickly', 'monotonous . . . more lilt in the voice'.

Presenting and simultaneously appraising youself can be difficult when you have an uncertain list of worries. The solution is, if possible, to rehearse your talk in front of someone who can give you useful feedback, or record what you say and listen to it critically. If you can pick up and correct any distracting mannerisms, or any tendencies to pepper your speech with potentially irritating 'errms' or 'you knows', in advance, you'll have a lot less to worry about once you're on.

Rehearsing in front of a constructive trial audience will give you vital feedback. Ask them:

- Did I grab the audience's attention from the start? Was my welcome and introduction OK?
- Do I look relaxed and in control?
- Do I talk clearly and concisely? Did I sound soporific?
- Do I use my visual aids well and do they fit in with the flow of my speech?
- How far back can the visuals be seen and can I be heard?
- Is it the right length?

Your list of self-management worries will obviously be personal and depend on the circumstances. Whatever it contains, keep it in the back of your mind as you begin.

TIPS

The key is to read the audience as you go.

- If your witty anecdotes are falling flat, drop them.
- Are your cue cards keping you on course? Or have you been diverted, now constantly having to look down at your notes and losing eye contact? Learn from every situation, don't panic.
- Be ready to cut out some of the presentation or change direction if the audience seems bored. Watch their body-language.
- Keep a close eye on the time – is the presentation running to schedule? If not, start cutting it down. Make sure you have a watch or clock with you.

When to arrive

❝ I always try to get to the venue early. This is to make sure the room is set up how I like it and to get a feeling for the likely atmosphere. Best of all, though, is that it gives me time to chat to the audience over coffee – get to know them and for them to see me as a human being. It usually makes things go well. ❞

– **Kay Fleming**

THE BIG DAY!

The last thing to do on the day is to arrive breathless and in a panic. Leave plenty of time to get to the venue – consider the traffic, road hold-ups, rail strikes or delays. If you do arrive in the nick of time, try to have your talk re-scheduled or calmly explain to the audience why you are a little flustered. Getting the audience on your side works wonders!

> **Allow yourself ample time to comfortably finish your set-up.**
>
> - Get to the venue early – if necessary the night before.
> - Try to get some rehearsal time in the room where the presentation will take place.
> - Talk to the technicians (if any) about your requirements. Have you got everything you need?
> - Set up and check all equipment carefully. If it's not your own, take time to learn how it works – even things like the flipchart easel. Load slides well before you start.
> - Mingle with members of the audience and greet them as they arrive.

TIPS

Checking the room

" *I try to get to know the room before a session begins. I ask myself: 'Where will I be standing?' 'How will the audience be seated?' 'Where is the equipment and can I use it from where I am standing?'* "
– **Jane Filey, personnel officer**

There are some standard room checks that are worth doing before a presentation. This is your chance to pre-empt any problems.

> **Look around the room and ask yourself:**
>
> - Will I need a microphone?
> - How effective is the blackout if I need it?
> - Where are the electrical sockets – do I need extension leads?
> - How can I control the heating or air conditioning?
> - Will there be a lot of traffic noise or any other distractions?
> - Are we likely to be interrupted?
> - Is the seating layout what I want?

TIPS

Seating layout is important in creating the right atmosphere. In some cases you will have little say in how the audience is seated. In that case you'll have to make the best of it. Be prepared to help the audience move to where they can see you and your screen/charts etc.

If you do have some flexibility in seating plans, here are some useful seating layouts to try:

- *Theatre style – rows of seating, useful for formal presentations to large numbers.*
- *Semi-circles – effective in creating a more informal atmosphere where discussion is encouraged.*
- *Boardroom layout – good for small group discussions and brain storming.*
- *'V'-shaped layout – more informal than theatre style, suitable for medium-sized audiences needing to look at the speaker and screens.*

ACT!

> When checking the room beforehand, put yourself in the position of the audience – will they be comfortable, can they see everything easily, have they got enough space to make their own notes? Take action if you see a problem.

> " *Being relaxed is essential in any presentation. The more you appear to be in control, and happy to be there, the more the audience will warm to you. And that makes things so much easier.* "
> **– Jane Filey**

Being relaxed means being in control. Being in control is vital in a presentation. If you are confident that you have checked everything, it will help you relax. With a couple of minutes to use your nerve-busting techniques and focus your mind, you're ready to roll.

Dealing with awkward customers

> " *The one recurrent nightmare even the most experienced presenters have is the difficult or aggressive questioner. Awkward questions often come from someone who likes the sound of their own voice or wants to show off, but sometimes it is a genuine concern.* "
> **– Les Rodriques, planning consultant**

THE BIG DAY!

> What will you do if a member of the audience fires an awkward question at you, one that you cannot or should not answer?

The main defence is to be prepared. Be ready for the difficult question or annoying member of the audience. There are effective tactics you can use.

> Here are some stock rejoinders you can try.
>
> - Thank the questioner but say: 'This is outside the scope of our talk today but I will happily discuss it with you after the session'.
> - Acknowledge the question and ask the questioner (or the audience) for his/her (their) opinion – 'That's a good question. What's your view/does anybody else have any ideas on this?'
> - With a straight face say: 'I'm sorry, I don't know the answer to that, but I'll find out for you'.
> - Keep it light. Try a little humour to get and keep the audience on your side – something like: 'I knew things were going too smoothly this morning, that's a very tough question.'
> - Say that all questions will be dealt with at the end. This buys you some time to think.
> - If somebody criticises your presentation, remind them that they've not heard it all yet.

The key is to *look* in control at all times. Even if you haven't a clue about the question, stay calm and try to get back on course as quickly as possible.

Planning a presentation in a hurry

> " *Sometimes, I have to give a presentation with only 24 hours' notice. The main thing is not to panic but to follow a simple set of procedures. It works every time.* "
> – **Dan Grey, language trainer**

fifty-five

PERSUASIVE PRESENTATIONS!

Here is Dan Grey's technique for planning a last-minute presentation:

- Set aside 90 minutes thinking and planning time.
- Note down as many ideas as you can think of – quantity not quality at this stage.
- Go through the list and cross out anything that is not essential or desirable.
- Put your points into an order, so they tell a story, and make up cue cards to lead you through it.
- At the very least have an introduction, development and conclusion.
- Make some simple OHP transparencies to hammer home your main points. (You could also do this with a flipchart but, if your handwriting is poor, type up the text points and photocopy on to OHP film.)
- Try to include at least two graphics (e.g. charts, cartoons, graphs).
- Use a flipchart so that when key points emerge during the presentation you can note them down.
- Do a quick room and equipment check before you start.

Tips for the big day

You've prepared meticulously. It's the day of your presentation.

1. Arrive at the venue early – allow plenty of time to set up and check your equipment (or learn how to operate what's already there).
2. Talk to the venue management about lighting, heating, ventilation. Make sure it suits your needs and you know how to use it.
3. Check the room. Will your audience be able to see and hear everything? Can you see any potential problem areas that need to be attended to?
4. Is the seating plan what you want? Rearrange it if not – it's a key part of creating the right atmosphere.
5. Set aside some time to rehearse if you can – practice makes perfect.
6. If you get the chance, meet and greet your audience. This is a great way to break the ice before you start.
7. Before you go on, give yourself a couple of minutes to bust your nerves and gather your thoughts.

THE BIG DAY!

> 8. Make sure you monitor yourself. Keep a discreet eye on the time so you stay on schedule – make cuts if you need to. Make sure your voice remains steady and interesting. Appear calm and confident.
> 9. Establish eye-contact with the audience. Read their body-language. If they are shuffling, eyes downcast, change direction and try to raise the tempo. Cut if you need to.
> 10. Be ready for the awkward question. Deflect it as calmly as possible. Try to stay on the course you want.

TIPS ✓

If you have prepared fully and you follow these simple but field-tested tips, you'll have no trouble on your big day. Knock 'em dead!

PRESENTATION PLANNER

Chapter 6

Given the vast range of possible types of presentation, we can't cover everything here. However, there are some elementary rules which apply to all kinds of presentation. This section gives you a step-by-step check list to use in planning any forthcoming presentation. Remember, the secret of a persuasive presentation is planning ahead.

If your presentation needs to be reasonably complex, you should ideally allow yourself two weeks for planning.

As well as identifying what preparation you need to do, you should work out a realistic schedule for when you will have completed the various elements.

The message

Every presentation must have a clear objective and you should believe fully in your message. You will not be convincing unless you know why you are giving this presentation and appear fully committed to what you are saying.

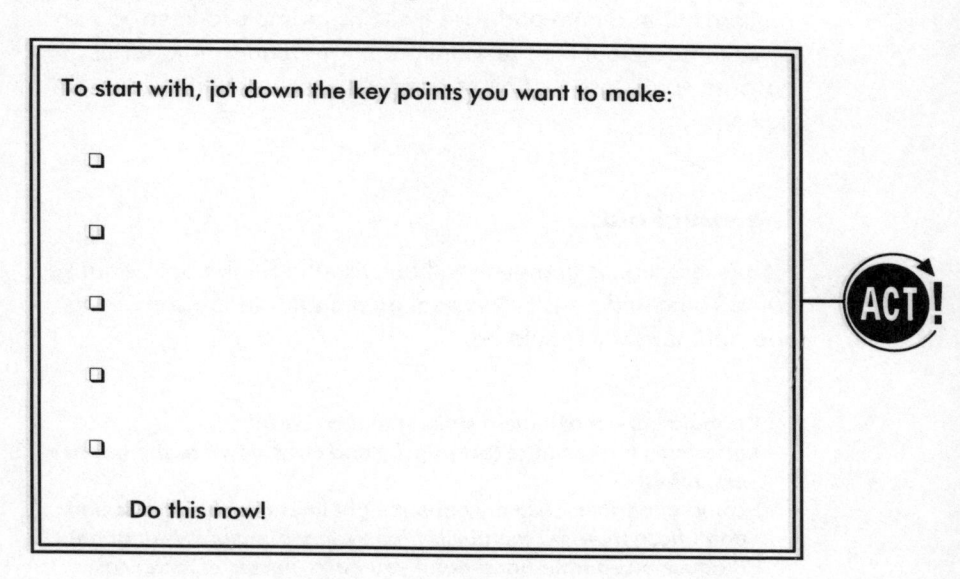

To start with, jot down the key points you want to make:

- ❏
- ❏
- ❏
- ❏
- ❏

Do this now!

This list should then be fleshed out and rearranged so it falls in the right order. Think of your presentation as a story – it should have a beginning, a middle and an end.

PERSUASIVE PRESENTATIONS!

Next, edit your draft carefully. Things to bear in mind at this stage are:

- *the level* – find out who will be in your audience and make sure you are not being patronising or too technical;
- *cut out as much as possible* – waffle will kill the audience's interest; brevity will make them love you;
- *make it as personal as you can* – relevant anecdotes about yourself can warm up the audience;
- *find an arresting opening* to grab the audience's attention.

ACT!

Find out about your audience

- ❏ *What will they be expecting?*
- ❏ *How can you supply it?*

Target completion date _____

After you have a final draft, write down the key features in order on cards or in a note pad. Use these as prompts to keep you on course throughout the presentation. Never read from a script because you'll lose that all-important eye contact with your audience.

The visual aids

No presentation is complete without visuals. Think about what key points you could transfer to visual media and design something appropriate. They should be:

- *stimulating* – make them striking and colourful;
- *informative* – keep the text punchy and cut it down to the barest essentials;
- *comprehensible* – use only about eight lines per sheet/slide and don't flash them up too quickly (one every 5 minutes is enough). Produce a separate hand-out if you have masses of technical detail to get across. Avoid clutter.

Your choice will obviously depend on the length of your presentation and the equipment you have at your disposal.

PRESENTATION PLANNER

> Decide on suitable visuals to reinforce your key points and make sure you have the appropriate equipment.
>
> - *Bullet-point summaries – slides/overhead projector.*
> - *Complex diagrams and photographs – slide projector.*
> - *Charts which build up during the course of your presentation – OHP/flipchart.*
> - *Lists built up with audience feedback – OHP/flipchart/whiteboard.*
>
> Target completion date _____

The venue

Make sure you find out about the room in which you're going to be giving your presentation. Your persuasiveness will not be enhanced if you turn up with a microphone and amplifier, slide projector and OHP, and then find that there's only one power point and no adaptors are available.

> Visit the venue if you can, or speak to the managers. Find out whether it has limitations which will affect your plans.
>
> - *Will you need a microphone to make yourself heard?*
> - *Can you black out the room enough to use a slide projector?*
> - *Will the back row of the audience be able to see your flipchart?*
> - *Will you have enough room?*
>
> Target completion date _____

PERSUASIVE PRESENTATIONS!

This is a task you should do as early as possible to avoid having to go back to the drawing board after dedicating a lot of time to preparation.

The equipment

Don't let your equipment become an embarrassment. Learn how to use it properly.

ACT!

> **Practise using all of the equipment beforehand.**
>
> ❏ Can you get your slides and OHP film the right side up and right way round every time?
>
> ❏ Can you erect your screen without giving a slapstick show?
>
> ❏ Does your flipchart easel stay upright as you rip off sheets with great gusto?
>
> ❏ Do your marker pens work?
>
> Target completion date _____

Simple things can make you look doltish – don't let them.

Rehearsals

It will help enormously if you can rehearse your presentation in front of a neutral audience. From their feedback you will find out whether:

○ *you can be seen and heard from everywhere in the room;*
○ *your message comes over strongly;*
○ *your visuals are effective;*
○ *you can use your equipment in the way you'd planned.*

PRESENTATION PLANNER

> A rehearsal is by far the best way of picking up any flaws in your presentation. Try to persuade friends or colleagues to watch you and criticise constructively. At the very least, tape yourself and play it back.
>
> Target completion date _____

ACT!

Remember, the more planning you put in, the more persuasive your presentation will be.